Christmas with Victoria

Volume VII

Text by
Jennifer Ciegelski

Oxmoor
House®

HEARST COMMUNICATIONS, INC.

Christmas with Victoria Volume VII

Copyright © 2003 by Hearst Communications, Inc.,
and Oxmoor House, Inc.

Oxmoor House, Inc.
Book Division of Southern Progress Corporation
P.O. Box 2463, Birmingham, AL 35201

ISBN: 0-8487-2737-1
ISSN: 1093-7633

Printed in Singapore
First printing 2003

We're here for you!
We at Oxmoor House are dedicated to serving you with reliable
information that expands your imagination and enriches your life.
We welcome your comments and suggestions. Please write us at:
Oxmoor House, Inc.
Christmas with Victoria
2100 Lakeshore Drive
Birmingham, AL 35209
To order additional publications, call (205) 445-6560 or visit us at
www.oxmoorhouse.com

For *Victoria* Magazine
Editor in Chief: Margaret Kennedy
Creative Director: Cynthia Hall Searight
www.victoriamag.com

Editor: John Smallwood
Designer: Curtis Potter

Produced by Smallwood & Stewart, Inc., New York City

FOREWORD 9

chapter one
INSPIRED BY NATURE 10

How to turn the boundless colors, shapes, and textures
of nature into beautiful, one-of-a-kind holiday decorations

chapter two
THE GIFT OF GIVING 34

Imaginative ways to make all your gifts special, from
beautiful papers and handmade gift tags to decorative containers

chapter three
MAGICAL TOUCHES 52

Use your favorite ornaments and create new ones
to enhance every corner of the house

Contents

chapter four
GRACIOUS GOODNESS 68

Make the kitchen a center for wonderful homemade gifts—
flavored vinegars, chocolate truffles, preserves, cookies, cakes, and more

chapter five
HOLIDAY DINING 78

Prepare a luxurious holiday feast with this simple and sophisticated menu—
and set a table as enticing and as special as the food you're serving

chapter six
SEDUCTIVE SWEETS 90

Sumptuous reinterpetations of holiday favorites
and delicious new desserts

RECIPES 100

PROJECTS 134

RESOURCES 140

For all the changes happening around us, there's something especially reassuring about tradition and ritual, and no more so than at Christmas. I take great pleasure and comfort in doing much the same thing every year: catching up with friends through cards and letters, decorating the house with precious ornaments that have been hidden away for months, gathering my extended family for dinners that revolve around treasured recipes.

And yet, at the same time, one of my greatest holiday delights is reinterpreting those very traditions and rituals. For me, finding new ways to keep the wonder and magic of the season alive can be as simple as wrapping my presents with special papers and ribbons, or choosing all new colors for the tree and table decorations, or designing and making my own place cards and gift tags.

Victoria Christmas is filled with just such ideas to keep your holiday traditions fresh and personal and always magical. It's all much easier than you might think. Join us on these pages, and we'll show you how.

Peggy Kennedy

EDITOR IN CHIEF, *VICTORIA*

chapter 1

Inspired by Nature

NATURAL WRAPPINGS
ORNAMENTS FROM NATURE
A GARDEN INDOORS
RETHINKING WREATHS
DRIED FLOWERS AND PODS
GIFTS TO THE GARDENER

Wherever the season may find you—surrounded by snow at an old country house or woodsy cabin, basking in the sun at a seaside cottage, or even in a city apartment—why not look to the boundless colors, shapes, and textures of nature for your holiday decor? Designs drawn from nature

enliven a home at any time of year, but most especially in midwinter. Winter greenery can take many forms beyond beloved holly and pine and fir Christmas trees, garlands, and wreaths—consider using miniature potted trees and plants; fragrant clippings of eucalyptus, boxwood or bay leaves; or fresh herbs such as rosemary and thyme. Branches of orange bittersweet or pink pepperberry add accents of color; various twigs, barks, and vines offer rustic charm. With a little paint or snips of twine, pods and pinecones and shells you may have collected throughout the year are transformed into ornaments that will hold their own against traditional glass decorations.

Unstructured beauty In nature, nothing is perfect, so decorate with a free hand. A simple wreath of cedar and seeded eucalyptus (opposite) presides above a mantel. Scallop shells underneath a cloche and a dangling starfish (above) are mementos from a vacation. Preceding pages: A clam basket is filled with starfish varieties and loops of natural cord awaiting their metamorphosis into ornaments for the tree. The table is laid with the same mix of greenery used on the mantel.

seaside celebration

Gifts of the deep Celebrate in a palette of sea blues and decorations inspired by underwater treasures. To dress each place setting, make instant napkin rings (left) by gluing scallop shells onto twine and tucking in a sprig of bay leaves. Better than coins in your stocking or a single Christmas star are these genuine sand dollars and dried starfish (below), their bleached-out color a wonderful take on winter white. Try inking them and hand-printing patterns on plain butcher paper to make your own gift wrap, or paint them gold or silver and hang them on the tree with twine. Sprigs of fragrant eucalyptus and bay leaves extend beyond the mantel and join seashells to decorate window ledges (opposite).

Artful gift wrap creates excitement about the secrets within

Whuen your holiday decor draws its theme from nature, gifts wrapped in brightly colored papers tied with shiny satin ribbons tend to look out of place. A softer palette, and softer material, are better choices. Papers A visit to a fine stationery store will uncover a variety of handmade wrapping papers textured by fibers, leaves, and flower petals (opposite, top left). Or you can make your own papers using appliquéd pressed flowers or inked imprints of leaves, seashells or bark. Wide rolls of brown kraft paper or white butcher's paper provide the perfect canvas. Toppers Like a star on the tip of the tree, a topper is something no gift should be without. Nature's idea of a good one might include a seashell (opposite, top right); a pinecone, a sprig of holly, herbs, or other greenery; even a walnut adhered with a knot or a bit of glue. Ties In lieu of fancy colored ribbons or metallic cords, secure your packages with yardage in more unusual choices such as raffia, twine (gardener's, butcher's, or waxed varieties), rickrack, colored yarn, twill hem tape, seam binding, and thin rope (opposite, bottom left). Tags Use leftover materials—even scraps of corrugated cardboard—to design your own gift tags and greeting cards. Embellish the papers with sprigs of winter greenery (opposite, bottom right), shells, berries, twigs, or pressed flowers in keeping with your theme.

Natural Selections

Borrow these palettes and accents from nature for your gifts.

Garden Combine greens with pastel yellow or pink yarn and add silk or crepe paper flowers, velvet leaves, paper insects.

Harvest Use deep red and gold hues embellished with wheat stalks, dried gourds, rough twines, or grapevines.

Seaside Choose a spectrum of blues and sandy shades dotted with shells, sand dollars, starfish, bits of driftwood, and twine.

Woodland Stay with a palette of dark greens and browns accented with pinecones, birch bark, hollies, cinnamon sticks, and sprigs of bittersweet.

Magical transformation With a little imagination (and some white paint), backyard or forest finds become delightful decorations. A spiraling wisteria pod turns into an icicle (right), while a pinecone, an acorn, and milkweed pods join to form an angel trumpeting a song on high (below). Learn how to make a Pinecone Angel for your tree on page 134.

Naturally adorned A tree trimmed in natural ornaments has an understated elegance that one decorated with store-bought decorations rarely has. This stunning study in white and gold (opposite) mixes classics such as blown-glass balls and teardrops with handmade wisteria-pod icicles, pinecone angels, painted leaves, and starbursts made from sweet-gum balls injected with dozens of toothpick rays. Beneath the tree are piles of gifts wrapped with handmade papers containing leaves and sprigs of greenery alongside twisty brown orbs hand-woven from Virginia creeper.

ornaments from nature

Growing concerns Devoted gardeners need not feel blue at the end of the growing season. There are plenty of activities to undertake indoors that will satisfy all green-thumbed urges. A sunny window is an ideal spot to establish an indoor garden (opposite). Outdoor ornaments such as statuary and gazing balls that might be forgotten in the snow and ice can watch over plants and bulbs inside. Gather pods and seeds throughout the season for holiday projects like this handsome Nut Topiary (right) dotted with dried rose hips and hazelnuts. You'll find the instructions to make the topiary on page 135.

Forcing bulbs

Flower bulbs are marvelously engineered to survive in the frozen earth through the winter. With a little work you can trick their inner timing mechanism into sending out beautiful flowers ahead of schedule to brighten any corner during the holidays.

Amaryllis and paperwhite narcissus are forcing favorites, because they don't require a period of chilling before planting. Hyacinth, tulips, and daffodils need to be kept cold for a time in order to simulate the winter; if you're an exerienced gardener you can cool them yourself, although it's much simpler to buy "pre-cooled" bulbs. If you buy and plant in mid- to late fall the bulbs should be in bloom by Christmas. The planting procedure is the same for all, although details like the size of the pot will change according to variety.

Arrange the bulbs in a well-drained pot with two inches of soil, or a watertight container with two inches of gravel, then add more soil or gravel to come up to the top of the bulbs. Plant very close together for the best display. Don't worry about overcrowding, as a tightly-packed pot will make a dazzling display when the flowers are out. Keep the container in a cool place until shoots begin to show, then transfer to a warmer spot where the bulbs will get indirect light.

After they begin to flower, it's best to remove the bulbs from direct light so they stay in bloom longer. If your bulbs bud too early, the process can be slowed by moving pots to a cool, dark place.

rethinking wreaths

Even the plainest cedar or pine wreath can be made exciting. Weave in other greens such as ivy and holly to give it more visual flair and add sprigs of bittersweet or other berries for color. A few dried roses or hydrangeas will also add variety. The simple holiday wreath can be rethought in dozens of ways. Shape Recall your principles of geometry to form a square wreath like this one made of long-lasting Spanish apple surrounding a mirror (opposite, top left), or try an oval, a triangle, or whatever shape suits your fancy.

Color While green might be the first color that pops into your mind, it's not the only one. A fresh or dried wreath in an unexpected hue such as a brilliant red (opposite, top right) preserves the feeling of the season and catches the eye anywhere it is placed. Think of amaranth, bittersweet, winterberry, or pepperberry as colorful options. Components Don't stop at greenery clippings—a wreath composed of objects such as pinecones (opposite, bottom left), jingle bells, glass ornament balls, millinery fruit, or velvet leaves is equally festive. Fragrance Evergreen and pine are fragrant symbols of Yuletide, but herbs such as rosemary (opposite, bottom right) and fresh eucalyptus are delightful alternatives to scent your home.

Sturdy Foundations

It's quite simple to make a wreath, especially when you have a good form as a base. Here are the most basic styles available at crafts stores:

Foam A lightweight base on which to glue beads, candies, or ornaments. Florist's foam can be soaked in water and used as a base for a live flower arrangement.

Straw Provides a full, rounded base to which organic elements such as leaves, dried flowers, nuts, and pinecones can easily be pinned or glued.

Wire Designed to be a sturdy enough support for heavy clippings such as evergreens, which are wired to the base. Available in single-wire (for thin wreaths) or double-wire (for lush wreaths).

A wreath's beauty may be fresh and fleeting or dry and everlasting

Layered approach The mantel is a virtual stage for a dioramic fantasy of greenery and flowers during the holidays. While you can layer the greenery as much as you like, one dominant element should stand out. For this rustic brick hearth (opposite), an urn is filled with a wild assortment of cut greens. Red winterberries and an amaryllis provide bright accents of secondary color, and additional branches and beloved objects such as a bee skep, a moss obelisk, lotus pods, and vine orbs fill out the mantel shelf. Below, a colorful mix of red, orange, and gold roses is accented with pinecones, juniper cuttings, and rosehips. The architecture of the mantel is underscored with a fringe of leaves; you may try a similar lineup using galax, lemon, or magnolia leaves.

lush assemblages

Fruits and foliage Instead of fresh flowers, use the colors and textures of fresh and dried fruit to enliven seasonal foliage. An arrangement in a large urn (right) juxtaposes evergreen cuttings with lady apples, dried orange slices, hypericum berries, and some vivid red dahlias. If you don't have the time or the inclination to create layers on the mantel, a singular arrangement like this one is a stunning substitute—and easy to clean up once Christmas has passed. Don't have a fireplace to decorate? No room for a full-size tree? An elegant tabletop topiary (below) will provide a focus for holiday cheer in a different way. This one is built on a base of live ivy and is dotted with lady apples, orange Chinese lanterns, bicolor roses, and viburnum berries.

fruitful additions

Graced with vines Needing little arrangement to look good, vines, twigs (opposite), and berried branches such as bittersweet, winterberry, and holly can be used to introduce lacy, natural forms thoughout the house. Try twining vines around a banister, a chandelier, table legs, or the back of a wooden chair or drape them around doorways or windows. This unusual sconce (below), created from an old wirework frame and a dish of beeswax candles, is dressed for the holidays with strands of bittersweet.

branches and vines

dried flowers and pods

It's a myth that the beauty of the garden is fleeting. There are many varieties of flowers and plants that can be dried and preserved and used in holiday decorating projects in the deepest days of winter. Here are a few of our favorites. **Swags** A variation on the wreath and garland, swags are lovely, indoors or out, at the corners of a window or doorway. This version (opposite, top left) features branches, herbs, and eucalyptus punctuated with the soft, dusty pink of dried garden roses and a cluster of pepperberry. **Kissing balls** As the name implies, this spherical decoration (opposite, top right) is often hung in doorways in lieu of mistletoe as a place to steal a kiss. It's easy to make with several dozen dried rosebuds secured in a foam ball. Simply hang it from a pretty ribbon. **Garlands** Use fresh greenery to provide the base for a garland, and add natural dried elements for texture and color. This harvest-themed version (opposite, bottom left) has accents of dried gourds, oak leaves, wheat sheaves, and ponderosa pinecones. A second garland of drilled and strung nuts is draped over it. **Gift accents** A dried flower, cinnamon sticks, or nuts are enchanting toppers on a gift. If you don't have a perfect dried specimen but would still like that natural look, try to find faux designs crafted out of fiber or paper, like this magnolia blossom (opposite, bottom right).

Drying Methods

Collect elements from your garden all year to use in your holiday decorating and dry them in a cool, well-ventilated place, such as a potting shed or garage, for several weeks.

Flowers Harvest roses, hydrangeas, lavender, and other flowers when they aren't damp from rain or dew. Hang them upside down so they dry straight.

Gourds Wipe clean of soil or any garden debris and dry on sheets of newspaper. To use, just drill a small hole through the neck.

Leaves Oak, maple, and magnolia leaves all preserve beautifully. For best results, layer between sheets of newspaper and press under a stack of books.

Pods Hang lotus pods, nigella, thistles, Chinese lanterns, silver dollars, and other everlastings upside down from their stems.

At their peak, dried flowers and pods become spectacular ornaments

THE FLOWERS

... en. I had the combination,
... storehouse at pleasure. No
... ock butterfly at his work. The
... fly brings pollen he will deposit
... inent pistil; then, thrusti...
... la in search of sweets,...
... gled in some of th...
... elf he ...
... pol-
... horde to an... cious
The sket... ... s
and two st... green ... nd
the one el... the ... an
pulled, doc...

Among ... human beings, some odd
... man in famili...

WILD FLOWERS
Every Child Should Kno...
by
FREDERIC·WILLIAM·ST...

THE LUPIN

FIELDBOOK OF
AMERICAN TREES
AND SHRUBS

F. SCHUYLER MATHEWS

No...

PLATE XIII

PLATE XIV

1. HONEYSUCKLE
3. RA...
2. MOUNTAIN EVERLASTING
... COMFREY

OUR
T...
BY HA...

A·WOMAN'S
HARDY·GARDEN

HELENA·RUTHERFURD·ELY

46a

46. Akelei — Aquilegia vulgaris L.
a) Wald-Akelei, b) Garten-Akelei (5 Arten)

HENDERSON'S HANDBOOK OF PLAN...

Natural imagery Any green thumb will be delighted by the gift of botanical prints of favorite plants (right) or a vintage garden book. Often full of exquisite engravings, sketches, and color illustrations, old garden volumes (opposite) are artistic treasures. Wrap these gifts simply in translucent glassine paper or green florist's tissue so decorative images show through, then tie with florist's twine.

Gifts for gardeners

Gardening is such a popular pastime that there are plenty of themed gifts you can select and create.

Flower press Encourage the preservation of favorite blooms with this thoughtful tool. Include a blank scrapbook to store the pressings.

Heirloom seeds Seed exchanges nationwide now source hard-to-find seeds for heirloom varieties. Sign up a friend for a membership, or create a personalized set of seeds for her or him to try.

Journal Every gardener needs a permanent place to record planting schemes and seasonal changes. Choose a beautiful blank book and inscribe the recipient's name on the flyleaf.

Forcing kit Gather some forceable bulbs (try amaryllis, narcissus, or hyacinth) along with a special vase designed for forcing (or a glass dish at least 3 inches high on the sides with stones for the roots to take hold). Place in a brown bag and tie with twine. See page 21 for more detailed forcing instructions.

Gloves and boots Odds are that every serious gardener either loses or wears out his or her gloves every season. Treat your friend to a brand-new pair, along with some colorful rubber garden boots or shoes.

Timeless treasures Search flea market or antiques shops for garden-themed gifts: colorful vintage seed packets for framing, old watering cans or florist's frogs for flower arrangements.

chapter 2

The Gift
of Giving

VELVET-CUFFED STOCKINGS
PATTERNS FROM THE PAST
GRAPHIC WRAPS
CLEVER CONTAINERS
FRAMED MEMORIES
RIBBON PORTRAITS
FRAGRANT SACHETS

patterned papers

Patterns from the past The elegant script of old handwritten documents makes for captivating wrapping paper with some simple photocopying. Letters, postcards, ledgers, recipe cards, or sheet music found at flea markets and antiques stores, or your own sketches can be turned into wrappable art. Even vintage wallpaper or fabric swatches can be "repurposed" in this way (below). For an old-fashioned touch, tear the edges of the photocopied papers and use sealing wax (left) or decoupage snippets and found images to dress up a simple giftbox (opposite). Instructions for making a decoupage box are on page 137.

Paper palettes The patterns may vary widely but choosing gift wrap in coordinating colors creates a unified look underneath your tree. For these grown-up presents (opposite and right), chic black and white are all over—in wide stripes, polka dots, harlequin diamonds, and handcrafted handwriting designs created on a photocopier. Accent colors of vibrant green and yellow on the satin ribbons and tags take their cue from the ornaments on the lovably straggly tree.

Scheming in color

Keeping seasonal color combinations simple is a reliable formula for success—especially on the tree, where too many colors can cancel each other out. When in doubt, keep to a single color—say gold or silver for the tree—then use a contrasting palette for all your gift wrap and ribbons. Here are some alternative pairings to traditional red and green.

Black & White If you're creating your own papers, look to the graphic appeal of dominos, playing cards, toile, etchings, stripes, and checkerboards as inspiration. Keep things lively by using ribbons or gift tags in accent colors of hot pink or red, citrusy greens, yellows, and oranges, or silver and gold.

Blue, Silver & White At this time of year, the world outside clothes itself in icy winter hues. Let the frosty colors of twilight skies, stars, icicles, and snowflakes inspire your choices of colors and patterns for wrappings and decorations.

Ivory & Gold You may already have ivory and gold elements in your decorating scheme in the way of serving pieces and vases; play them up for the holidays, or enhance their innately dressy quality with subtle touches of red and green.

Pink & Pistachio This pairing is an updated, feminine interpretation of the more traditional red and green of the season—and softer on the eye.

clever containers

Christmas cones The concept of the favor cone dates back to Victorian times. These days, such nostalgic receptacles are perfect for small gifts or edible treats. Dangling from a branch on a Christmas tree (left) or sharing space with other ornaments in a pretty compote (opposite), they are decorative, too. Paper cones like the vintage-themed ones at left are simple to make. You can embellish them with cutouts of found images or photocopies of illustrations from vintage cards or children's books. The rose cone was simply made from a photocopy of a ladies' handkerchief. Turn to page 138 for the instructions.

Glamorous gift bags As the holiday party tempo picks up, a gift of wine or spirits for your host may be just the thing to keep the celebration going. Bottles can be awkward to wrap with paper, so a more beautiful (and reusable) option to conceal your gift would be a fabric bag (right) tied with a ribbon or tasseled cording. With basic sewing skills, you can make your own; you'll find instructions on page 139.

Seasons
Greetings
from, Devorah

Gallery gift Creating an art gallery (opposite) for a friend is easier than it may seem—the "artworks" are color photocopies from books and the "frames" are ribbon. Scour used bookstores for volumes of interest (right), then photocopy the images on sturdy paper. Choose brocaded, embroidered, and ruched ribbons in colors to complement the art. A steady hand and some fabric glue is all it takes to create the borders. For added durability, mount the prints on foam-core board before applying the ribbon.

Suitable for framing

Flea markets, used book stores, and tag sales are good sources for old prints, postcards, and magazines to turn into framed gifts.

Animal books Look for biology classifications or prints by masters such as Audubon. Try varied images of a single animal—dogs, birds, fish, or butterflies.

Architectural drawings Renderings of famous buildings make a lovely series, as do classical elements such as columns, pediments, and statuary.

Botanicals Peruse out-of-print garden books or horticultural manuals for frameable images of flowers, leaves, trees, herbs, fruits, and vegetables.

Images for kids Create framed art for a child you know with illustrations and text from vintage books of nursery rhymes, ABCs, or fairy tales.

Fabric patterns Photocopy interesting fabric swatches or even colorful vintage scarves or antique ladies' handkerchiefs.

Fashion illustrations Check out fashion magazines from the early twentieth century to find charming drawings of the looks of the day.

Maps Even an armchair traveler would appreciate a collection made from old school atlases, travel guides, and road maps of favorite destinations.

well-loved decorations

Past perfect Some of the most heartwarming gifts and decorations are vintage classics, made by hand in a whimsical, primitive style. Don't overlook these beauties when rummaging through flea markets and tag sales, and be sure they're passed along to good homes where their time-worn beauty will be appreciated. Here, a hand-painted snowman sign (above) and a jointed Santa toy (right) serve yet another year on their new owner's Christmas tree.

chapter 3

Magical Touches

MANTEL FINERY
TIMELESS TREASURES
WINDOW WONDERS
THE ESSENCE OF
HOLIDAY SPARKLE
PRECIOUS STILL LIFES

Christmas is a time to decorate with abandon. Passionate collectors of holiday ephemera rediscover their treasures each December with glee, but even the most reserved among us can't resist the urge to deck our halls with special tokens of the season. Let your boughs be laden with ornaments in

a multitude of sizes, shapes, and colors. Dress every mantel with an enchanting mix of greenery, flora, and a few little surprises to admire while you sit by the fire. Compose a colorful tabletop still life inspired by your favorite collection. Create the illusion of icicles indoors with an assortment of sparkly ornaments hanging in a window. If there's no room on the tree, fill glass bowls or vases with surplus ornaments and place them on window ledges, bedside tables, or in entrance halls. Drape swags of colored glass beads around mirrors or windows. Through these decorations, displayed with affection and care, we create lasting memories for our friends and family to treasure and beloved traditions we welcome year after year.

Holiday hues Sophisticates might fancy metallics (opposite), and elegant arrangements in silver, bronze, and gold. For traditionalists, Christmas wouldn't be the same without red and green. There are always new ways to use them—to infuse ordinary glass vases with holiday red, simply fill them with cranberries (above) or colored marbles. Preceding pages: Ornaments resembling sugared fruits are just a few of the gems on a life-size feather tree spilling over with treasures.

mantel finery

Natural hearthscapes The mantel is second only to the tree as the focal point for holiday decorations. For harmony, choose a unified color scheme for both. Flanked by winter-white floral arrangements and dressed with boxwood, an architectural mirror (left) reflects flickers of mercury glass votives and silver candlesticks. A rustic stone hearth (below) sets a stage for a rhythmic march of diminutive evergreens and red roses interlaced with cranberry garlands. An unadorned magnolia wreath (opposite) strikes a woodsy tone of muted browns and greens. Decorative pairs of hurricane lamps and pinecone wreaths bring a pleasing symmetry to the mantel composition.

timeless treasures

Collecting old-fashioned ornaments for the tree can be a year-round pastime, whether you seek newly minted baubles or vintage examples. For added interest, chose a theme to guide your hunt; here are a few of our favorites. FIGURES & FAUNA Ornaments modeled after St. Nick are, of course, a given, but you might also look for other characters of the season including snowmen, polar bears, reindeer, and angels (opposite, top left). DESTINATIONS & LANDMARKS Travelers of both the real and armchair varieties are charmed by souvenirs of buildings and icons from around the world—how about a clock tower or windmill (opposite, top right) bobbing from the branches of your tree? CHILDREN & TOYS It's no surprise that ornaments in the shape of hobby horses, drums, alphabet blocks, nursery-rhyme characters, and even children themselves (opposite, bottom left) are so popular, especially with kids. FRUITS & VEGETABLES Some of the earliest European blown-glass ornaments imitated the bounty that families hoped to reap throughout the year. New and old ornaments in the form of fruit baskets (opposite, bottom right) and cornucopias, as well as oranges, apples, bunches of grapes and nuts, are all readily available.

Vintage Collectibles

Be on the lookout for pieces of holiday history at tag sales and antiques stores.

Dresdens Made from the 1880s until World War I, these hand-painted, gilded, embossed cardboard decorations were once very popular but are now rare. Three-dimensional versions probably held candy.

Feather trees Made from goose or chicken feathers, originals from the 1890s to the 1940s are rare; a few companies now produce similar trees.

Kugels Introduced to the United States from Germany around 1880, these silvered glass orbs quickly became very popular. Larger versions were probably intended to hang in windows or doorways.

Lametta Silvery tinsellike tufts on a flexible wire base were fashioned into garlands and ornaments. Old pieces are very fragile but have a lovely tarnished patina.

New and old become beloved heirlooms

Light fantastic If the tree overflows with ornaments, send extras to the windows, where they can glimmer like indoor icicles. Those made of colored glass, crystal, or mirrors will catch the bright-white light reflected on the snow outside. Even droplets from a chandelier or beaded strands from a glass necklace can be used to shimmering effect. Thread the ornaments securely with snippets of ribbon or metallic cording tied to a curtain rod, and remember to stagger their lengths so as to help prevent collisions.

window wonders

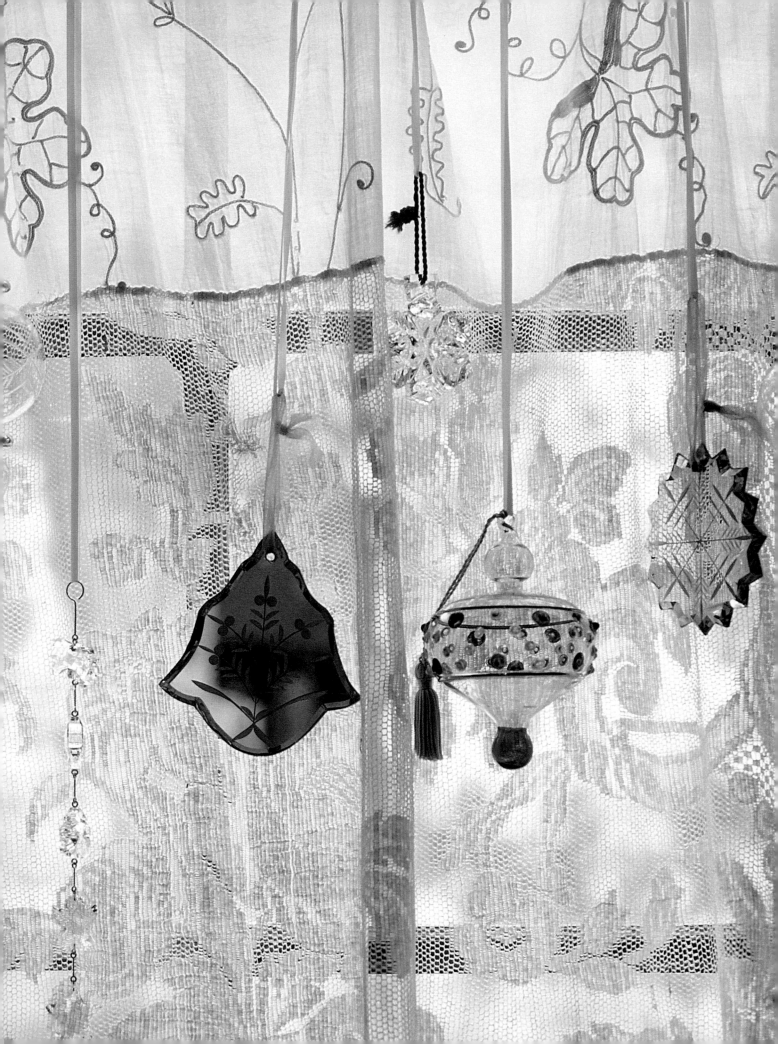

Magical mirrors Like a sleight-of-hand artist, you can play many tricks with mirrors. Add one or several to a room decked in holiday finery and everything is instantly multiplied and more festive. Use mirrors' reflective powers to enhance the shimmering intensities of candlelight, as this peephole mirror does with tall tapers and votives (right). Hanging small looking glasses as if they were art (opposite)—especially when the frames themselves are artful—is a wonderful way to dress up a plain space. Choose complementary sizes and styles (these are all gold-leafed) and securely attach them to wide ribbons.

The essence of holiday sparkle

Looking for a way to light up gray days and chilly evenings? Even without a roaring fire, here are easy ideas for adding a little magic to your home.

Candles Votives, pillars, and tapers are inexpensive ways to create a warm, intimate environment filled with soft, ever-changing light. To create instant atmosphere, dim the electric lights, then group candles generously, or put out singles to enliven dark hallways, powder rooms, and other unexpected places.

Crystal Now is the time to bring all your best pieces out of hiding. Crystal candlesticks and goblets call to mind winter's ice. Pile blown-glass globe ornaments into bowls and compotes.

Mercury glass While true mercury is no longer used, modern reproductions abound in silver and metallic colors. Look for candleholders, serving pieces, and butler's balls to highlight your tables and mantels.

Mirrors Propped on a living room mantel or hung above a dining room buffet, full-size mirrors reflect the energy around them tenfold. Lay smaller mirrors flat on a tabletop and place flickering votives or seasonal arrangements on top to multiply their effect.

Silver With company coming, by all means polish up your good silver and put it out on display. Candelabras, julep cups, coffee sets, and serving pieces lend instant glamour to casual and formal celebrations alike.

precious still lifes

For a truly personalized twist on holiday decorating, consider surrounding yourself with a show-and-tell of the things you love. Your collection need not be lavish or even expensive; just try to make sure the palette or the overall design of the objects contributes to the merriment in your home. FESTIVE PATTERNS A good pattern adds a jaunty note to a room. If you're lucky enough to have several pieces of tartanware (opposite, top left), you know that its red and green colors seamlessly meld with traditional holiday decor. Items with polka dots or multicolored stripes would also be effective accents. SPARKLING JEWEL-TONES Garnet, emerald, sapphire, amethyst—colors borrowed from gemstones lend unique richness. One source might be etched-glass or cut-crystal vases, decanters, or goblets (opposite, top right). SHIMMERING METALLICS The luster of silvered or colored mercury glass catches and reflects light beautifully. The vases, candlesticks, and gazing balls in this grouping (opposite, bottom left) date from between 1860 and 1920. COLORFUL IMAGERY Collectors may flaunt a full service on the table for Christmas dinner, but unused tureens and odd platters and teacups in floral or architectural themes are lovely in their own right. This collection is mostly English Staffordshire (opposite, bottom right).

Ways to Display

Make your treasured collection the center of holiday attention; just be sure it's well out of harm's way.

Centerpieces Smaller collections are particularly suited to serve as conversation starters at the center of the dinner table. Delicate objects can be placed on a pedestal cake stand to keep them above the action.

End tables A dim hallway, dark nook, or lonely corner is instantly brightened by the addition of a small (but sturdy) end table piled high with colorful crystal serveware, a bowl of blown-glass Christmas ornaments, or a grouping of sterling silver.

Shelves Bookshelves, wall niches, windowed armoires, curio cabinets, and hutches help protect precious pieces while still keeping them on view for all to enjoy.

Cherished collections on view for the holiday show

Dining room dressing Dress up your dining area and tabletop with decorations in multiples: In this room (right), a coordinated series of objects works together to set a lovely scene. Why stop at one large wreath in the window when you can display several scaled-down ones? On the table (below), forgo a traditional solitary centerpiece and opt for a succession of smaller arrangements mingled with candles high and low.

numbers game

chapter 4

Gracious
Goodness

PRECIOUS PRESERVES
SWEET BITES
CONES OF COOKIES
SPICY SESAME SOY NUTS
CHOCOLATE DECADENCE

From the spicy scent of fresh-baked gingerbread cookies to the savory aroma of a roasted goose, the kitchen is the fragrant focal point of any holiday preparations. Why not make it a center for gift-giving as well? Luscious creations from your kitchen can be remarkably easy

to make and package, and they bear the warmest and most personal of greetings. For one- and two-bite treats such as cookies, chocolates, and candies, think in quantity: Don't even bother making a mere handful—beyond those you'll be giving as gifts, you'll no doubt be indulging in a few tastes yourself! Set aside a quiet afternoon, revisit favorite family recipes, and try the new ones you'll find in these pages. Your efforts in the kitchen are sure to find an appreciative audience, from the hostess of a Christmas cocktail party to a loved one far away. Select packaging suitable for the gift within—secured with colored ribbon, even everyday kitchen wrappings such as cellophane and fluted paper can get in the holiday spirit.

Jeweled jellies Jams and jellies sparkling in clear glass jars (opposite) are always welcome gifts. Try seasonal combinations such as Cranberry and Blood Orange Conserve (above), presented in a lacy Moroccan tea glass. Preceding pages: We've tucked a handful of Hazelnut Gems into a tiny tote, and poured a sampling of Herb and Cranberry Vinegars into crystal cruets. Turn to pages 132, 131, and 133 for the recipes.

sweet bites

Cookie cornucopias A cone is a perfect little holder for bite-size, buttery Christmas cookies (left). To make your own, simply twist and tape a square of heavy silver or gold paper into shape, then line it with wax paper. Finish by gluing on a snippet of cord or ribbon and a tiny ornament as a special Christmas keepsake.

Truffle favors No trifles, these truffles (opposite). When tucked into shimmering organza bags (lined with cellophane) and piled on top of a trio of cakestands, they become delectable gifts for guests. The dark-chocolate nuggets are perked with peppermint and lightly dusted with cocoa. Turn to page 128 for the recipe. Their live counterparts may be poky, but these chocolate caramel turtles (right) will practically scoot off the plate. For a hostess gift, include a pretty dish, such as this creamware one, to double the delight. Enclose in cellophane and tie with patterned ribbon. The recipe is on page 125.

Sweet and savory surprises Adults who crave cookies will be thrilled to receive a grown-up take on their favorite treat. These sophisticated Chocolate Espresso Cookies (opposite) are doubly indulgent—the chocolate batter is intensified with espresso and chunks of bittersweet chocolate. Pack them carefully in cupcake papers in a colorful tin so they arrive intact at their destination. Turn to page 130 for the recipe. Nuts are as much a part of the holidays as cocoa and candy canes. For a spicy snack, Sesame Soy Nuts (right) have a delicious flavor that will ensure they won't last long. Turn to page 102 for the recipe.

Under Wraps

Bags Dress up plain brown paper bags with festive tags, ribbon, or holiday stickers, or create your own from fabric scraps cut with pinking shears and gathered together at the top with a brightly colored ribbon.

Baskets Baskets are ideal for gifts with multiple components. Assemble a kitchen basket of edible gifts and useful implements for a cook, for example, then line or wrap baskets with tea towels or pieces of fabric, or fill them with excelsior or shredded paper.

Boxes Cookies and candies are at home and safe in white bakery boxes, wooden boxes in different shapes, or even Chinese food containers. Embellish with greenery, glitter, or ink stamps.

Jars Decorate with a gummed label on the lid or front of the jar to let the recipient know what's inside. Cut a cap of fabric with pinking shears; hold it in place with ribbon or waxed twine.

Papers A smart choice for a range of edible goodies, especially buttery loaves or cakes. Choose from wax paper, parchment paper, or kraft or butcher's paper. Tie with colored string or patterned ribbon.

Tins Essential for keeping cookies and crackers crisp and chocolates and fudge fresh. Round tins in Christmas colors are classic, but don't overlook vintage versions you might find in an antiques store. Simply line them with a few folds of wax paper.

Chocolate choices Anything made with chocolate is always welcome. Studded with dried cherries, this Chocolate Brioche Loaf (below) may be light in texture but it is rich in flavor—a tantalizing tea loaf. You can substitute dried cranberries for a tangy seasonal flavor. To pattern the parchment paper wrapping, try a special paper punch, as we did, or an embosser. The cupcake "knots" of this festive Yule log, or Bûche de Noël (opposite), mimic a real tree. It's made like a layer cake; no rolling is required. The fun is sculpting icing along the edge to look like bark, the top as tree rings. Turn to pages 126 and 124 for the recipes.

decadent delights

chapter 5

Holiday Dining

GOOD BEGINNINGS
TABLE GRACES
NEW YEAR'S SUPPER
SUMPTUOUS SIDE DISHES
SAY CHEESE

One of the best things about Christmas is the time we get to spend with those we love. Out-of-town relatives come in for a visit, and friends drop by for company and conversation. We welcome them all warmly into our homes, often to sit down together to share a holiday feast:

Good beginnings Welcome guests with a few savory nibbles that will stimulate their appetites, such as these Spicy Pecans and Miniature Caramelized Onion Tartlets (opposite); the recipes are on page 102 and 103. Warming Apple-Rutabaga Soup (above) dressed up with whipped cream is a delicious prelude to the main attraction; turn to page 104 for the recipe. Preceding pages: Our turkey is first soaked in a flavorful herbal brine, then roasted; the recipe is on page 112.

nourishment for all the senses as the comforting sounds and smells from the kitchen fill the house. This is the time to set a table as generous and rich and special as the food we're preparing. Select the linens, china, and silverware and plan the seating arrangement and decorations well in advance. If possible, get the table ready ahead of time—between cooking and attending to guests and family you may not have a lot of time on the day. Don't hold anything back—everything should speak of warmth and bounty and festive spirit. Layer your best linens for even greater effect, bring out your crystal; personalize each place setting with a different mix of seasonal greenery, small ornaments, and fresh fruit.

table graces

Starting with Thanksgiving dinner and continuing through a drowsy-but-jovial brunch on New Year's Day, the holiday table is the center of much activity and good cheer. And in the same way we decorate the tree for the season, we can dress the table for these occasions as well. DISHWARE If you have a set of fine china (opposite, top left)—a wedding gift, perhaps, or handed down from your grandparents—now is certainly the time to use and enjoy it. You might also look for interesting patterns at estate sales and assemble a mix-and-match table in a charming jumble of designs. Chargers, platters, and tureens can all be put to good use with your holiday menus. LINENS Tablecloths, runners, and napkins in Yuletide colors or patterns instantly put any table in the spirit. Accent each napkin with a special token (we used a mother-of-pearl buckle opposite, top right), a tiny ornament, or a few inches of ribbon or tasseled cording. GLASSWARE When you're ready to raise a toast with a fine vintage or some bubbly, set the table with special glassware (opposite, bottom left) such as flutes, goblets, and wine glasses in crystal, blown glass, or even colorful cut-glass designs. PLACE CARDS They may seem old-fashioned, but cards (opposite, bottom right) are an effective way to help guests find their seats easily, add another decorative element to the table, and enable the hostess to arrange for lively conversation.

Place Cards

Go beyond the standard tented card and show your guests to their seats with style.

Favors Attach place cards to a little something for guests to take home: a candy cane, a piece of marzipan or chocolate candy, a tiny ornament.

Holders Tuck place cards into decorative stands or tiny picture frames, or use small pine cones or lady apples as card stands.

Supplies While plenty of preprinted cards are readily available, you can easily make your own. Choose sturdy papers and embellish them with ink stamps or a picture of the guest. Cut with pinking shears, and handwrite the names in ink with a flourish.

A handmade place card is a thoughtful welcome

New Year's Supper

Pasta in Champagne Sauce
with Golden Caviar
Crown Roast of Lamb
Wild Rice Pilaf
Spiced Beet Medley

When only a special few are on the guest list for a sophisticated New Year's Eve celebration, choose a menu that raises simple dishes to sheer elegance. Our pasta with caviar is impressively luxurious, yet it's completely affordable and requires minimal effort to prepare. To make sure you're not too busy to join in the fun, set up a buffet with something special—we suggest a crown roast of lamb—as the dramatic centerpiece accompanied by savory side dishes with an unexpected twist. After dinner, serve a special dessert and pour cordials or Cognac while you reflect on the year that's passed.

A cozy gathering This New Year's Eve, start with something surprising but totally in keeping with the spirit of the occasion, such as Pasta in Champagne Sauce with Golden Caviar (above), recipe on page 111. Then move on to the meaty masterpiece, an impressive Crown Roast of Lamb stuffed with Wild Rice Pilaf (opposite), recipes are on pages 113 and 109. Serve the accompanying Spiced Beet Medley in a glass dish to put the glorious gold and ruby colors on display, recipe on page 106. Ready for another course? Go European style with a salad following the entree (left). This crispy concoction of mixed greens surprises the palate with slivers of aged goat cheese, chopped walnuts, and juicy pomegrante seeds.

choosing sides

L ike supporting actors to a star, side dishes are often unsung heroes. Yet a holiday feast just wouldn't be the same without them. Whether you're cooking an entire meal at home or asked to bring along a dish to a dinner party, you'll want to prepare sides that add dimension to the meal. Here are four delectable re-interpretations of classic side dish themes. BREADS If biscuits and rolls feel too commonplace, opt for something with savory style. These Cornmeal Madeleines (opposite, top left) are flavored with buttermilk and a hint of rosemary. The recipe is on page 128. GRATINS What hides beneath a gratin's golden-brown crust? A seductive mix of butter- and cream-infused vegetables. Here (opposite, top right), the traditional potato is joined by its root sisters the turnip and the carrot. The recipe appears on page 107. VEGETABLES Some greens round out the offerings and add color to the table. The secret to these room-temperature Brussels Sprout Petals à la Grecque (opposite, bottom left) is a piquant vinaigrette. Find the recipe on page 105. STUFFINGS While every family has its favorite, if you're looking to try something new, sample individual portions of custardy Bread Pudding Stuffing with Onion Cream (opposite, bottom right). Our recipe is on page 110.

Simple Choices

With a few extra ingredients, these familiar winter staples are transformed into delectable side dishes that would grace any meal.

Brussels sprouts Toss with butter and lemon zest, chopped toasted nuts, or freshly-grated Parmesan cheese.

Carrots Toss with butter or olive oil; add chopped ginger and grated orange zest, brown sugar or maple syrup; or mix with some dried cranberries and toasted pecans.

Onions Try cipollini or pearl varieties. Halve and roast in olive oil; sprinkle with chopped thyme or sage, or balsamic or sherry vinegar.

Potatoes Roast in olive oil with sea salt and chopped rosemary, or mash with roasted garlic and fresh parsley.

Sumptuous sides are tailor-made for second helpings

With fruit The salty-sweet pairing of cheese and fruit is a very satisfying punctuation to a meal, served either French-style (after salad, before dessert) or the British and American way (following dessert). Ripe Bosc pears poached in port temper the richness of Maytag blue cheese wedges (opposite), while grilled apricots and raisin-bread rounds sweeten a mild, soft ricotta (right). The recipes are on page 129.

With cake Dried fruits such as figs, dates, cranberries or apricots are also a fine accompaniment to cheese. Rich and chewy slices of dense Date Nut Cake (left) are a perfect contrast to a creamy Italian mascarpone sprinkled with nutmeg. The only thing missing is a glass of fragrant dessert wine. The recipe is on page 122.

chapter 6

Seductive

Sweets

BREAKFAST WREATH
FROZEN PUMPKIN SOUFFLE
HEAVENLY SLICES
DREAMY CRÈMES
BLOOD ORANGE TARTLETS

Heavenly slices Chocolate lovers will swoon at the very sight of this frilly Black Forest Cake (below). Underneath its seemingly prim exterior hides a decadent pairing of chocolate mousse and Chantilly cream punctuated with sour cherries. This Spiced Plum Gingerbread Cake (opposite) also holds a secret—in addition to its heady mix of ginger, cinnamon, cloves, and nutmeg, the batter is flavored with plum tea to lend a subtle sweetness. The simple confectioner's sugar icing, too, is infused with plum tea, which turns it a lovely pink. Recipes on pages 120 and 125.

baked treats

Dreamy crèmes Use the edge of your spoon to gently crack through its golden, caramelized crust, then dip into the rich, creamy center. This is no ordinary bistro dessert, but a luscious tropical version—Coconut Crème Brûlée (opposite). The ingredients of a classic Pot de Crème (right) are surprisingly simple—heavy cream, whole milk, egg yolks, and sugar—but the end result is irresistibly rich and custardy. We've flavored this one with flecks of vanilla beans, but you may want to try cocoa or coffee. These French desserts are best made in individual servings—no sharing necessary. Turn to pages 115 and 117 for the recipes.

Crème brûlée flavorings

Citrus A teaspoon or so of grated lemon, lime, orange, or even grapefruit zest will contribute a wonderfully tart edge to this creamy dessert. Whisk into the eggs before adding to the cream.

Coffee Coarsely ground espresso beans, together with a small amount of very strong coffee, gives crème brûlée a caffeinated boost. Stir these ingredients into the cream as it is heated on the burner.

Spices A ginger crème brûlée is easily made by adding a few tablespoons of very finely chopped crystallized ginger to the cream before heating. For cinnamon crème brûlée, stir 1/2 to 3/4 teaspoon ground cinnamon into the strained custard.

Liqueurs For orange crème brûlée, add about 2 tablespoons of Grand Marnier to the custard before pouring it into the ramekins. Almond-flavored amaretto will also give subtle enhancement, or add two tablespoons each of bourbon and dark rum and a pinch of nutmeg for an eggnog version.

Vanilla In this classic crème brûlée, a vanilla bean, split to expose the seeds, is added to the cream as it heats; the bean is removed, leaving the seeds behind. If vanilla beans are not available, vanilla extract is an acceptable substitute; use only pure vanilla extract, of course; add 1 1/2 teaspoons to the strained custard.

fruitful encounters

Fresh Greens Nestled into an etched-glass compote, these bite-size slices of fruit (left) glisten like precious gems. Kiwi pieces, halved green grapes, honeydew melon balls, and star fruit slices get their sheen from a coating of fragrant jasmine tea cooked in lime sugar syrup. A dollop of green-tea ice cream would continue the tea theme and match the palette of the dessert. You'll find the recipe on page 122.

Tarts of Christmas If a chocolate or custard dessert seems to be too rich of a finale to a holiday feast, think of the refreshing taste of a fruit tart. These zingy little Blood Orange Tartlets (opposite) are infused with orange juice as well as grated peel. They wear a delicate lattice of meringue and are accompanied by pâtes de fruits. Buttermilk Ice Cream is a soothing contrast to the intense flavors of a harvest-inspired Apple, Pear, and Dried Plum Tarte Tatin (right). The recipes are on pages 119 and 118.

Recipes

The recipes in this section are listed below alphabetically for easy reference. The page number for the photograph is given first; the page number for the recipe is given second, in italics.

apple, pear, and
dried plum tarte
tatin
98, *118*

apple-rutabaga
soup
81, *104*

black forest cake
94, *120*

blood orange
tartlets
99, *119*

bread pudding
stuffing with onion
cream
87, *110*

breakfast wreath
92, *123*

brine-cured roast
turkey
78, *112*

brussels sprout
petals à la grecque
87, *105*

bûche de noël
77, *124*

buttermilk
ice cream
98, *114*

chocolate
brioche loaf
76, *126*

chocolate
caramel turtles
72, *126*

chocolate fudge
sauce
90, *114*

chocolate hazelnut
madeleines
91, *128*

coconut crème
brûlée
96, *115*

cornmeal madelines
87, *108*

cranberry and blood
orange conserve
71, *132*

cranberry salsa
132

cranberry vinegar
69, *133*

crown roast
of lamb
84, *113*

dark chocolate
peppermint truffles
73, *128*

double chocolate
espresso cookies
74, *130*

frozen pumpkin
soufflés
93, *116*

fruits in jasmine
tea syrup
98, *122*

grilled apricots
89, *129*

hazelnut gems
68, *131*

herb vinegars
69, *133*

miniature
carmelized onion
tartlets
80, *103*

pasta in champagne
sauce with golden
caviar
85, *111*

pears poached
in ruby port
with rosemary
88, *129*

potato gratin
with turnips
and carrots
87, *107*

pots de crème
97, *117*

spiced plum
gingerbread cake
95, *125*

spiced beet medley
84, *106*

spicy pecans
80, *102*

spicy sesame
soy nuts
75, *102*

sweetened spiced
mascarpone
89, *122*

wild rice pilaf
84, *109*

SPICY SESAME SOY NUTS

3 tablespoons soy sauce

2 tablespoons Asian sesame oil

1 tablespoon unsalted butter

2 teaspoons honey

1 teaspoon sea salt

3 cups roasted unsalted nuts

1 1/2 tablespoons toasted sesame seeds

1/8 to 1/4 teaspoon cayenne pepper,
or to taste

Is it possible for nuts to become even nuttier? When you coat them with sesame oil and toasted sesame seeds, the answer is a resounding yes. Pass these around as a complement to cocktails. These spicy nuts tickle the tongue with their flavorings of cayenne pepper and honey. We like to use a gourmet mix of pecans, cashews, and almonds, but the Asian-inspired seasoning will be delicious on whatever nuts you fancy.

1. Preheat the oven to 350°F. In a large bowl, combine the soy sauce, 1 tablespoon of the sesame oil, the butter, honey and salt. Add the nuts, sesame seeds and cayenne pepper and toss to coat. Spread the nuts on a baking sheet and bake, stirring once, for 15 to 20 minutes, or until golden brown and fragrant. Add the remaining 1 tablespoon sesame oil, toss to combine, and let cool. Transfer to jars or containers with lids. Stored in a cool, dark place, the nuts will keep up to 2 weeks. Makes 3 cups.

SPICY PECANS

4 tablespoons unsalted butter

3 tablespoons sugar

2 teaspoons Cajun seasoning

2 teaspoons ground cumin

1/2 teaspoon cayenne pepper

1 pound pecan halves

Need a quick fix for last-minute entertaining? These spicy pecans take just a couple of minutes to prepare. Serve a bowlful warm with a wedge of cheese and some wine when unexpected guests come to call, or pack up a boxful to give to a friend.

1. In a large skillet over medium high heat, heat the butter until it begins to foam. Add the spices and sugar and cook, stirring, until combined. Add the pecans and cook, stirring, for 3 minutes, or until toasted.

2. Transfer the pecans to a wire mesh rack set over a baking sheet and let cool to room temperature. Store in an airtight container until ready to serve. Warm before serving. Makes about 4 cups.

MINIATURE CARAMELIZED ONION TARTLETS

FOR THE PASTRY SHELLS:

1 recipe of your favorite pie dough

FOR THE CARAMELIZED ONIONS:

2 tablespoons unsalted butter

2 medium onions, preferably Vidalia, thinly sliced

1 teaspoon sugar

Salt to taste

FOR THE CUSTARD:

3 large eggs

¾ cup heavy cream

2 tablespoons Dijon mustard

A pinch of celery salt

A pinch of cayenne pepper

The wonderful flavor and diminutive size of these French-style savory tartlets make them an excellent hors d'oeuvre for a cocktail party. Or, serve a trio of tartlets with a side salad to each guest as a light holiday lunch.

1. Make the pastry shells: Lightly spray 2 mini muffin pans with non-stick cooking spray. On a lightly floured surface, roll out the dough ⅛ inch thick. Using a 3-inch round cookie cutter, stamp out 24 circles of dough. Fill each muffin cup with a dough round, pressing it into shape. Line with paper, fill with pie weights and chill for 30 minutes.

2. Preheat the oven to 350°F. Bake the shells for 6 to 8 minutes, or until pale golden. Remove from the oven and allow to cool in the pans. When the shells are completely cool, invert the pans onto a baking sheet, then turn the shells right side up.

3. Make the onions: In a saucepan over medium heat, melt the butter. Add the onions and cook, stirring, until wilted. Reduce the heat to medium-low and cook, stirring frequently, until the onions are a rich gold. Add the sugar and salt and continue cooking until the onions are the color of brown sugar. Remove from the heat and set aside.

4. Make the custard: Whisk all the custard ingredients until well combined.

5. Preheat the oven to 350°F.

6. Assemble: Place ½ teaspoon caramelized onions in each pastry shell. Cover with the custard. Place the tartlets on a baking sheet. Bake for 10 to 12 minutes, or until the custard is just set. Makes 24 hors d'oeuvres.

APPLE-RUTABAGA SOUP

½ cup (1 stick) unsalted butter

1 cup coarsely chopped onion

1 cup peeled, cored, and coarsely
    chopped Granny Smith apple

1 cup coarsely chopped rutabaga

1 cup chopped butternut squash

1 cup coarsely chopped carrots

1 cup coarsely chopped sweet potato

Salt to taste

5 cups chicken stock

1 cup heavy cream

3 tablespoons maple syrup, or to taste

Cayenne pepper to taste

If you've ever encountered a rutabaga in the grocery store and ruminated on its possible uses, now is your chance to find out how good it can be. This large pale yellow root vegetable resembles a turnip and is actually a member of the cabbage family. Its mild flavor is the perfect partner to tart Granny Smith apples in this creamy soup. Serve the soup with the Cornmeal Madeleines on page 108 as a light lunch, or as part of a complete meal before Brine-Cured Roast Turkey (page 112), Bread Pudding Stuffing (page 110), Potato Gratin with Turnips and Carrots (page 107), and Brussels Sprout Petals à la Grecque (page 105).

1. In a large saucepan over medium-high heat, melt the butter. Add the onion, apple, rutabaga, squash, carrot, sweet potato, and ½ teaspoon salt and cook, stirring occasionally, until the onion is translucent. Add the chicken stock, bring to a boil, and simmer, stirring occasionally, for 30 to 35 minutes, or until the vegetables are tender.

2. Transfer the soup in batches to a food processor and process until smooth. Return to the saucepan, and add the cream, maple syrup, and salt and cayenne to taste. Bring to a simmer, stirring occasionally, and cook until heated through. Serves 8.

BRUSSELS SPROUT PETALS À LA GRECQUE

2 pounds brussels sprouts, rinsed

FOR THE VINAIGRETTE:

1/2 cup water

1/2 cup dry vermouth or dry white wine

1 onion, finely chopped

3 cloves garlic, minced

1 teaspoon white wine vinegar

1 teaspoon coriander seeds

1/2 teaspoon fennel seeds

3 tablespoons extra virgin olive oil

1 tablespoon fresh lemon juice

2 sprigs fresh thyme

1/2 bay leaf

1/2 teaspoon cracked black pepper

Salt and freshly ground pepper to taste

While you may have come to expect bright green little heads of brussels sprouts as a side dish during the winter months, here they are prepared with a twist. Not only are the sprouts served at room temperature, not warm, but the heads are separated into individual leaves, or "petals."

1. Bring a large pot of salted water to a boil. Fill a bowl with ice water.

2. Meanwhile, with a paring knife, trim the ends of the brussels sprouts and peel off the leaves one by one.

3. Add the brussels sprout petals to the boiling water and cook for about 20 seconds, or until they turn bright green. Do not overcook. Drain and refresh the petals in the ice water. Allow to chill completely, then drain and pat dry. Refrigerate until ready to serve.

4. Make the vinaigrette: In a saucepan over medium heat, combine the water, vermouth, onion, garlic and vinegar. Bring to a boil, then remove the pan from the heat and set aside.

5. Meanwhile, in a spice grinder or clean pepper mill, grind the coriander and fennel seeds. Add the olive oil, lemon juice, thyme, bay leaf, fennel, coriander, and cracked black pepper to the vermouth and vinegar mixture, stir, and cool to room temperature. Adjust the seasoning if necessary. The vinaigrette can be made up to 2 days ahead. Store covered in the refrigerator and allow to come back to room temperature before serving.

6. To serve: In a bowl, toss the brussels sprouts with the vinaigrette. Serves 8.

SPICED BEET MEDLEY

3 pounds assorted small beets—red, golden, and candy-striped (Chioggia), if available

4 tablespoons olive oil

1 teaspoon salt, or to taste

1/2 teaspoon freshly ground pepper, or to taste

1/8 to 1/4 teaspoon ground cloves, or to taste

1/8 to 1/4 teaspoon freshly grated nutmeg, or to taste

1/2 to 1 teaspoon ground coriander, or to taste

1 to 2 tablespoons sherry vinegar (available at specialty food shops)

This pretty side dish adds some color to the winter table. We recommend using a mix of different colored beets for the most impact. In addition to widely available dark purple or red beets, look for the sweet golden type and the white-and-red striped Chioggia variety.

1. Preheat the oven to 400°F.

2. Trim the stems of the beets to 1 inch and scrub well. Arrange them in a shallow baking pan large enough to hold them in one layer. Add 2 tablespoons of the olive oil and turn to coat. Bake for 45 minutes to 1 hour, or until the beets can be pierced easily with a knife.

3. Cool the beets until they can be handled, and remove the skins. Cut the beets into bite-sized pieces, keeping colors separate until serving time so that the darker beets will not discolor the lighter ones.

4. In a bowl, combine the remaining 2 tablespoons olive oil with the salt, pepper, spices, and vinegar. Drizzle over beets (in separate bowls) and toss gently. The beets can be prepared up to this point 1 day ahead; chill, covered.

5. To serve: If the beets have been chilled, let sit at room temperature for an hour. Transfer to a serving dish. Serves 6.

POTATO GRATIN WITH TURNIPS AND CARROTS

4 tablespoons unsalted butter

1 onion, thinly sliced

1 quart heavy cream

2 cups milk

2 tablespoons kosher salt, or to taste

1 teaspoon white pepper

Freshly grated nutmeg to taste

4 medium to large turnips, peeled and
   sliced 1/4 inch thick

4 medium to large potatoes,
   peeled and sliced 1/4 inch thick

6 medium-large carrots,
   sliced 1/4 inch thick

The addition of turnips and carrots lends a sumptuous sweetness to a classic French potato gratin. Warm and rich, it is a comforting treat on a cold winter's eve. Serve the gratin with the Bread Pudding Stuffing on page 110 and the Brussels Sprout Petals à la Grecque on page 105 as a series of side dishes for the Brine-Cured Roast Turkey on page 112.

1. Preheat the oven to 375°F. Butter a large shallow baking dish.

2. In a large casserole over medium heat, melt half the butter. Add the onion and cook, stirring occasionally, for 5 minutes, or until translucent. Add the cream and milk, bring to a boil, and season with the salt, pepper, and nutmeg. Add the turnips, potatoes, and carrots, folding them in with a spatula until completely coated. Simmer the vegetables until the cream begins to thicken and the vegetables are almost tender, about 8 minutes. They should not be completely cooked.

3. Transfer the vegetable mixture to the buttered baking dish and dot the top of the vegetables with the remaining butter. The dish can be assembled 1 day ahead; store in the refrigerator, covered.

4. Bake in the upper third of the oven for 15 to 20 minutes, or until the top is golden brown and the vegetables are tender. Serves 8 to 10.

CORNMEAL MADELEINES

6 tablespoons unsalted butter, softened

1/2 cup sugar

1 large egg, lightly beaten

1 1/4 cups all-purpose flour

1 cup plus 2 tablespoons cornmeal

1/2 teaspoon baking powder

1/8 teaspoon baking soda

1/2 teaspoon salt

1/2 tablespoon finely chopped garlic

1 tablespoon finely chopped fresh
rosemary

1 cup buttermilk

Fragrant with rosemary and garlic, shell-shaped cornmeal madeleines are a step above their common muffin cousins. Serve them as a side dish as part of a dinner featuring the Apple-Rutabaga Soup and Brine-Cured Roast Turkey on pages 104 and 112, or pair them with your own warming chowders, chilis, or stews.

1. Preheat the oven to 350°F. Spray two madeleine tins with nonstick vegetable spray.

2. In a medium bowl with an electric mixer, cream together the butter and sugar until light and fluffy. Add the egg and beat just until combined.

3. In another bowl, combine the flour, cornmeal, baking powder, baking soda, salt, garlic, and rosemary. With the mixer on low, alternately add the dry ingredients and buttermilk to the butter mixture, scraping the sides and bottom of the bowl occasionally.

4. Fill the madeleine molds halfway with batter. Bake for 5 to 7 minutes, or until golden. Let cool for 5 minutes and invert onto racks. Continue baking madeleines in the same manner with the remaining batter. Makes about 48 madeleines.

WILD RICE PILAF

3 tablespoons unsalted butter

2 leeks, white parts only, thinly sliced
and washed

2 carrots, finely chopped

1 celery stalk, finely chopped

1/2 cup dry sherry

1 1/2 cups wild rice

1 1/2 teaspoons salt, or to taste

1/2 teaspoon freshly ground pepper,
or to taste

1 cinnamon stick

3 cups vegetable or chicken stock or
canned broth

1/2 cup diced dried apricots

1/2 cup slivered or chopped lightly
toasted pistachios

Enhanced with the flavor of dried apricots and pistachios, this rice is a savory substitute for stuffing. When accompanying a Crown Roast of Lamb (see page 113), you don't even need a serving bowl. Simply spoon the rice into the enter of the roast before bringing it to the table— use any extra rice to garnish the platter along with sprigs of fresh herbs.

1. In a large saucepan over medium heat, melt the butter. Add the vegetables and cook, stirring occasionally, for 5 minutes. Do not brown. Add the sherry and simmer for 5 minutes.

2. Stir in the rice, salt, pepper, and cinnamon. Add the stock and bring to a boil, then reduce to a simmer. Simmer, covered, for 40 to 50 minutes, or until the rice is tender and most of the liquid is absorbed. Remove from the heat and stir in the apricots and pistachios. Remove the cinnamon stick and adjust the seasoning if necessary. Serves 6.

BRINE-CURED ROAST TURKEY

FOR THE BRINE:

3 1/4 cups sugar

1 1/4 cups kosher salt

2 cups honey

6 sprigs each fresh parsley, dill, thyme, tarragon, and sage

2 sprigs fresh rosemary

2 tablespoons mustard seeds

2 tablespoons fennel seeds

2 cinnamon sticks

5 bay leaves

8 whole cloves

1 tablespoon juniper berries

2 tablespoons whole black peppercorns

2 lemons, cut in half

1 tablespoon whole allspice berries

2 gallons boiling water

One 18- to 20-pound fresh turkey

1 pound unsalted butter, melted

"Curing" a turkey overnight in an herb-infused brine results in meat that is both flavorful and extremely moist. Be sure to use only a fresh turkey for this technique, however—frozen, self-basing, and kosher turkeys have already been salted, and the brine would make them too salty. You will need a container large enough to hold the turkey in the brine (and ample refrigerator space for the setup); if you don't have a large stockpot (or lobster pot), simply buy an inexpensive plastic wastebasket large enough to hold the bird. Otherwise, the procedure is simplicity itself, and the results wonderfully satisfying. If you like, decorate the serving platter with sprigs of rosemary to echo the woodsy flavor of the brine.

1. Combine the brine ingredients in a large container, pouring the boiling water in last. Stir to dissolve the sugar and salt, then let cool to room temperature. Add the turkey, cover, and refrigerate overnight.

2. Preheat the oven to 300°F.

3. Remove the turkey from the brine and rinse under cold water. Cover the entire turkey with cheesecloth and place in a large roasting pan. Using a brush, saturate the cloth with some of the melted butter. Roast for 3 to 4 hours, basting the cheesecloth with the butter every 30 minutes. The turkey is done when the thigh-joint temperature reaches 175-180°F.

4. Remove the turkey from the oven and let it rest for 30 minutes.

5. Carefully remove the cheesecloth and transfer the turkey to a platter. Serves 8 to 10.

CROWN ROAST OF LAMB

1 crown roast of lamb, consisting of 2 racks of lamb (14 to 16 chops), bones frenched

2 teaspoons coarse salt, or to taste

1 teaspoon freshly ground pepper

1 large navel orange, scrubbed

2 small heads garlic, cut in half parallel to the root end

1 large bunch fresh thyme

1 recipe Wild Rice Pilaf (see page 109)

Named for its shape, this roast is fit for a king (or, more likely, a special dinner for New Year's Eve). Ask your butcher to french the roast for you, trimming the little chop "handles" of all fat; you can even decorate their ends with paper frills, if you like. Once the roast has cooked, it can rest while a course of Pasta in Champagne Sauce with Golden Caviar (see page 111) is served.

1. Preheat the oven to 500°F. Place roast in a roasting pan and season with the salt and pepper. Stuff the orange into the center of the roast, to flavor it and help hold its shape. Place the garlic, cut side down, on top of the orange. Arrange the thyme sprigs between the chops and on top of the roast; reserve a few sprigs for garnish.

2. Roast for 10 minutes. Reduce the temperature to 350°F and continue to roast for 30 to 35 minutes more, or until the chops have reached an internal temperature of 125° to 130°F for medium-rare. Remove from the oven and let rest for 15 minutes.

3. Place the roast on a platter. Remove and discard the orange, garlic, and thyme. Spoon the pilaf into center of roast and garnish with the reserved thyme sprigs. Serves 4 to 6.

BUTTERMILK ICE CREAM

5 large egg yolks

1½ cups sugar

2 cups milk

2 cups heavy cream

½ vanilla bean, split lengthwise

1¼ cups buttermilk

While it may look like play-by-the-rules vanilla, this ice cream will surprise your guests with its piquant buttermilk flavor. Serve a scoop alongside a generous slice of the hearty Apple, Pear, and Dried Plum Tart Tatin on page 118 for a delicious dessert.

1. In the top of a double boiler placed over simmering water, whisk together the egg yolks and sugar until the mixture becomes slightly thickened and foamy.
2. Meanwhile, in a saucepan, combine the milk, cream, and vanilla bean and scald.
3. Slowly pour the hot milk mixture into the egg mixture, whisking constantly, and continue to cook over medium heat until the custard coats the back of a spoon. Remove from the heat, strain, and cool to room temperature.
4. Add the buttermilk. Freeze in an ice-cream maker according to the manufacturer's instructions. Makes about 1 quart.

CHOCOLATE FUDGE SAUCE

1 cup heavy cream

6 ounces unsweetened chocolate, coarsely chopped

⅔ cup sugar

⅓ cup light corn syrup

3 tablespoons unsalted butter

1½ teaspoons vanilla extract

A pinch of salt

Spoon this rich classic fudge sauce over an after-dinner piece of cake or scoop of sorbet—try a tart raspberry sorbet, the colors mix beautifully—for dinner-party guests or to top a yummy sundae as a midnight snack after an evening of wrapping presents. Any leftovers will keep for weeks.

1. In a saucepan, bring the cream to a simmer. Stir in the chocolate, sugar, corn syrup and butter. Simmer, stirring frequently, until the chocolate melts. Cook at a low boil for 5 minutes, stirring occasionally. Remove from the heat. Stir in the vanilla and salt. Transfer to a bowl and cool to room temperature.
2. When the sauce is cool, transfer to jars with tightly fitting lids. Store in the refrigerator for up to 1 month. Makes about 2½ cups.

COCONUT CRÈME BRÛLÉE

1 quart heavy cream

1 cup dried unsweetened (desiccated) coconut (available at specialty food stores or Indian markets)

1/2 cup vanilla sugar (or substitute 1 teaspoon vanilla extract and 1/2 cup granulated sugar)

9 large egg yolks

1/2 cup granulated sugar for the crust

While crème brûlée is decidedly French, this one has a tropical flair thanks to the flaky coconut hidden under its crispy crust. The secret to a luscious crene brulee is to use wide shallow molds—no more than 1 inch high—so the custard cooks evenly in the water bath and is a creamy and delicate contrast to the carmelized sugar topping. Broil about two inches from the heat with the door open so the custard doesn't cook further.

1. Preheat the oven to 300°F. Have ready 8 round crème brûlée molds, 1 inch deep by 4 inches in diameter.

2. In a saucepan over medium heat, combine the cream, coconut, and vanilla sugar (if using regular sugar, add the vanilla extract to the strained custard), bring to a boil and simmer over medium-low heat, stirring occasionally, for 30 minutes.

3. Meanwhile, in a large bowl, whisk the egg yolks. Strain the cream mixture into a large measuring cup and pour it in a stream, whisking, into the egg yolks. Strain again into the measuring cup and carefully skim the foam from the surface. Pour the custard into the molds and transfer them to a large baking pan. Add water to the baking pan to reach halfway up the sides of the molds. Bake for 1 hour or until just set. Remove molds and cool to room temperature.

4. Preheat the broiler. Sprinkle a thin layer of sugar on each crème brûlée. Place under the broiler until a golden-brown crust covers the surface, carefully turning the molds as necessary for even carmelizing. Serve immediately. Serves 8.

FROZEN PUMPKIN SOUFFLÉS

1 cup granulated sugar

1/2 cup water

6 large egg whites

1 quart heavy cream

2/3 cup confectioners' sugar

1 1/2 cups solid pack pumpkin

1 1/2 teaspoons ground cinnamon

1 teaspoon freshly grated nutmeg

1/4 teaspoon ground cloves

1/4 teaspoon ground allspice

1 tablespoon vanilla extract or the seeds from 1 vanilla bean

2 cups finely chopped toasted pecans

1/2 cup toasted pumpkin seeds

These individual soufflés will win over even the staunchest traditionalist at your holiday feast. All the flavors of the familiar pumpkin pie are here—cinnamon, nutmeg, cloves, and allspice— in a cool, creamy frozen custard. A garnish of toasted pecan and pumpkin seeds adds a crunchy counterpoint to the smooth cream. And, although these mimic the appearance of the classic hot soufflé, rising high above the tops of their ramekins, there is no need to worry about last-minute preparation—they can be made up to a day ahead (and they're guaranteed not to fall!)

1. Prepare the molds: You will need eight 6-ounce ramekins or soufflé molds. Cut two 14-inch-long sheets of parchment paper or waxed paper lengthwise into 2-inch strips. Wrap a strip around the outside of a ramekin to make a collar extending 1 1/2 inches above the top edge of the dish and secure with tape. Repeat with the remaining ramekins.

2. In a small saucepan over medium heat, combine the granulated sugar with the 1/2 cup water. Bring to a boil, stirring to dissolve the sugar, then cook, without stirring, until the sugar syrup registers 240°F to 246°F on a candy thermometer. Remove from the heat.

3. Meanwhile, in a large bowl with an electric mixer, beat the egg whites to soft peaks. Beating constantly, slowly pour the hot sugar into the egg whites in a thin stream. Once all of the sugar has been added, whip the egg white mixture on high speed until it is cool and forms stiff peaks.

4. Meanwhile, in a bowl, combine 3 1/2 cups of the heavy cream with the confetioners' sugar and beat until the mixture forms soft peaks.

5. In a large bowl, whisk together the pumpkin, the remaining 1/2 cup cream, cinnamon, nutmeg, cloves, allspice, and vanilla. Fold the egg whites into the pumpkin mixture. Then fold in the whipped cream until no trace of white shows.

6. Divide the pumpkin mixture among the ramekins, filling them almost to the top of the paper collars. Freeze for at least 6 hours, or overnight.

7. Remove the parchment-paper collars and roll the sides of the soufflés in the toasted pecans. Allow to sit at room temperature for about 5 minutes before serving. Garnish each with a few toasted pumpkin seeds. Serves 8.

POTS DE CRÈME

1 cup heavy cream

2/3 cup milk

2 vanilla beans, split lengthwise

4 large egg yolks

1/3 cup sugar

It's hard to believe how just a few simple ingredients—cream, milk, eggs, sugar, and vanilla—can result in such a luxurious and velvety dessert. In lieu of standard ramekins, a selection of mismatched vintage custard cups would be a pretty way to serve these pots de crème.

1. In a saucepan set over medium heat combine the cream, milk, and vanilla beans and bring just to a simmer. Remove from the heat and let infuse for 30 minutes. Then remove the vanilla beans; scrape the seeds into the cream mixture.

2. In a large bowl, with an electric mixer, beat the yolks with the sugar until the mixture is pale yellow and falls back into the bowl in a ribbon when the beaters are lifted. Whisk in the cream mixture and strain the mixture into a bowl. Let stand for 15 minutes, then skim the surface of all foam.

3. Preheat oven to 325°F.

4. Divide the custard among four 4-ounce ramekins. Place them in a shallow baking pan and add enough hot water to reach halfway up the sides of the ramekins. Bake, covered loosely with buttered foil, for 20 to 25 minutes, or until the sides are set but the centers remain jiggly. Let cool to room temperature and chill before serving. Serves 4.

The following is a chapter-by-chapter listing of sources for as many of the items pictured in this book as possible. Every effort has been made to ensure the accuracy of addresses, telephone numbers, and Websites, but these may change prior to or after publication.

INSPIRED BY NATURE

pages 10–17
Shells from She Sells Sea Shells, 1157 Periwinkle Way, Sanibel Island, FL 33957; (239) 472-6991

page 11
Screened garden lanterns from Paris Market Collection, Alda's Forever, www.aldasforever.com

page 12
Compote from English Country Antiques, P.O. Box 1995, Bridgehampton, NY 11932; (631) 537-0606

Shell sphere, papers from Loose Ends, 2065 Madrona Avenue S.E., Salem, OR 97302; (503) 390-2348

Bell Jars from Abigails, 3219 Industrial Street, Alexandria, LA 713301; (800) 678-8485

page 14 (top left)
"Casa Azul" cream soup cup and platter, "Casa Picco" salad plate, "Chambord" dinner plate, "Bernadotte" champagne flute and goblet from Villeroy & Boch, 35 Main Street, Southhampton, NY 11968; (631) 283-7172

page 15
"Alexa" 77-inch sofa in denim from Mitchell Gold, 135 One Comfortable Place, Taylorsville, NC 28681; (800) 789-5401

Shell prints from English Country Antiques, P.O. Box 1995, Bridgehampton, NY 11932; (631) 537-0606

page 16 (top left)
Paper from Loose Ends, 2065 Madrona Avenue SE, Salem, OR 97302; (503)390-2348

Raffia, from Raffit Ribbon, 1155 Shames Drive, Westbury, NY 11590; (516) 333-6778

pages 27
Stockings from Christmas Cove Designs, P.O. Box 128, Richmond, ME 04357; (800) 737-2128; www.christmascovedesigns.com

TOKENS OF JOY

pages 35
Ribbons, boxes, paper from Tail of the Yak, 2632 Ashby Avenue, Berkeley CA 94705; (510) 841-9891

page 37
Stockings from Clover Linen, (770) 266-5713

pages 40-41
Interior design by Stephen Shubel Design Inc., 11 Ross Common Ross, CA 94957; (415) 925-9332

"Taffeta Tabis" from Clarence House, 211 East 58th Street, New York, NY 10022; (800) 632-0076

Photo Credits

Quentin Bacon
pages 78, 79, 80, 81, 87, 93, 95, 98

Jim Bastardo
pages 25, 26, 27, 38 (top), 39, 137

Guy Bouchet
pages 66, 67

Susie Cushner
pages 8, 10–16, 34, 37, 42 (right), 60, 61

Richard Felber
page 65 (bottom right)

Sheeva Fruitman
page 3 (right)

Steve Gross & Sue Daly
pages 22 (top right), 83 (top left)

Bill Holt
pages 2, 3 (left), 33, 35, 40, 41, 43, 83 (bottom left), 138, 144

Charles Maraia
pages 9, 54–57, 63, 72 (right)

Jeff McNamara
pages 18–21, 23 (top and bottom right), 24, 28, 42 (left), 51(right), 52, 53, 59, 65 (top right), 134, 135, 139

Susan Gentry McWhinney
pages 65 (top right), 68, 69, 70, 71, 72 (right), 73–77, 92, 143

Rob Melnychuck
pages 45 (top right), 68, 70

Minh & Wass
pages 65 (bottom left), 88, 89

Steven Mark Needham
page 32

Toshi Otsuki
pages 29 (left), 31 (top right, bottom left, bottom right), 38 (bottom), 48–50, 51(top), 62

David Prince
pages 5, 90, 91, 94

Steven Randazzo
pages 1, 140

Michael Skott
pages 22 (bottom right), 45 (top left, bottom left, bottom right)

William Steele
page 31 (top right)

Ann Stratton
pages 84, 85, 83 (bottom right), 99, 100

Dominique Vorrillon
page 96

Alan Weintraub
pages 36, 136

Michael Weschler
page 97

Marlene Wetherell
pages 46, 47, 83 (top right)